Girls Know How®

Raising the Roof

Written by
Ellen Langas Campbell

Ellen Langas

Illustrated by April D'Angelo

A Kids Know How® Book

Kids Know How®
NouSoma Communications, Inc.

First printing 2005

GIRLS KNOW HOW® and KIDS KNOW HOW® are registered trademarks of NouSoma Communications, Inc.

ISBN-13: 978-0-9743604-1-6
ISBN-10: 0-9743604-1-4

LCCN: 2005900348

ATTENTION SCHOOLS AND ORGANIZATIONS: Quantity discounts are available on bulk purchases of this book for educational or gift purchases. Special books or book excerpts also can be created to fit specific needs. For information, please contact NouSoma Communications, Inc., 35 Founders Way, Downingtown, PA 19335, Ph 610-458-1580, books@nousoma.com.

Proud supporters of *Students In Free Enterprise*.

Contents

Dedicated to my mother, Angie Langas,
who, like so many mothers,
listens and listens…and listens!
I love you!

With appreciation to:
Sally Bovell, Dede Crough, April & Chris D'Angelo,
Dr. Pat McDonnell, Kendall Price, Gesine Thomson,
Upper Uwchlan Township and Rita Wilson

With special thanks to Linda Alvarado,
who graciously shared her inspiring story

Many thanks to our wonderful and spirited
group of "kid testers" and helpers:
Adrianna, Bill, Brittany, Glenn, Jamie, Jessica, Kelsey,
Maggie, Matt, Matthew, Michelle, Robert,
Stephanie and Veronica

1

Tori crouched behind a giant oak tree. Her heart was pounding so hard, she was sure it could be heard ten feet away. Slowly, carefully, she peered around the broad trunk. With a silent flick of her wrist, she signaled to Kelly and Angie, letting them know the coast was clear. Hiding behind a bush, the girls nodded, quickly got to their feet and sprinted to join Tori in a line behind the tree. They watched and waited in silence, catching their breath and planning their next move.

"Wait here," Tori commanded. "I'll run up to the water pump and let you know if it's clear."

"Be careful," cautioned Angie. Her wide eyes were filled with concern for her friend.

"Thanks. Okay, ready, set..." She peeked around the tree to see if it was safe to run.

Splat!

"I've been hit!" Tori shrieked as she covered her face with both hands and returned to safety behind the tree.

Angie and Kelly looked at their friend in surprise. "Argh!" they screamed in unison as they watched her contorted face. "Blueberries!"

A stream of dark slime dripped down Tori's face. The girls snapped to attention as more blueberry rockets were launched toward their hiding spot.

"Run for your lives!" yelled Kelly. They turned and fled, hearing the pounding feet behind them getting closer.

They ran as fast as they could, zigzagging around trees, jumping over stumps and snagging their clothes on bushes as they tried to dodge the flying fruit. In minutes, they were out of the woods and in the safety of their neighborhood. Their chasers stopped at the woods' edge, but the girls kept on running. Tori, sweating and streaked with blue, turned to see the boys, the tormenters, laughing and eating the blueberries that served as weapons just minutes ago.

There were four of them: Max, Ricky, Einstein and Ben. The boys turned and worked their way through the woods, following the trail of smashed blueberries.

"Did you see it? A direct hit!" boasted Max. He was just over five feet tall, the daredevil of the group.

"That should keep the girls out once and for all," said Einstein. Tall and thin, the brains and computer whiz of the group, his real name was George Dunmore. He was dubbed "Einstein" after he scored highest on the county math achievement tests for the fifth grade.

"Look!" said Max, as he used a stick to poke at a purple ponytail scrunchy in the leaves.

"Treasure!" agreed Einstein. "Pick it up and take it back to the clubhouse."

Within minutes the boys returned to the point where the battle began. It was a wooden clubhouse, the size of a one-car garage, with two windows and a front door. Prominently displayed above the door was a computer-generated banner with the words *BOYS RULE, GIRLZ DROOL!* The boys entered, filled with a sense of excitement and victory.

"Let's celebrate," announced Ricky as he produced a box of chocolate-covered doughnuts. The boys dug into the box. Ricky, whose full name was William Ricardo, took after his father, who was a craftsman and owner of Ricardo's Hardware in town. Ricky showed the boys how to add new supports to the roof and secure the door. He was always working on a project at home with his dad.

Ben was Einstein's little brother. He didn't talk much, and he didn't cause much trouble. At age seven, he was just happy to tag along with the fifth-grade boys.

Max handed the scrunchy to Ben, who knew

exactly what to do. Walking over to a large box with a metal combination lock, he carefully turned the knob on the lock to the right, then the left, then the right, using the numbers he had memorized. *Click,* and the lock was open. He lifted the lid of the box that contained a pen, a silver dollar, an ace of clubs playing card and two arrowheads. He proudly placed the scrunchy on top, closed the lid and locked the box.

The clubhouse was about six feet high with a tin roof that kept the rain out, except for a few leaky spots. Inside, the floor was simply packed dirt with a straw mat cover.

The boys were all from the same neighborhood. Ricky's and Max's dads had both been born in Coreyville and remembered the clubhouse from when they were kids. It had gone through many transformations as different groups called it their own. But for now the four boys were its rulers, and that meant respect and admiration from the kids in the neighborhood.

It wasn't long ago that this rugged boys' hangout was decorated with blue and white-checkered curtains and freshly painted flower boxes hanging from the windows. It was enough to make a boy shudder.

2

Flushed and out of breath, the girls reached Tori's home. Tori was already five feet tall, lanky and a little awkward. She had blonde hair that hung just above her shoulders. She had lived with her dad since her parents divorced when she was four. Her mother lived in London, and she visited during summer vacation and winter break.

Mrs. Blair, a retired librarian, came to the house each afternoon to watch her until her father came home. Whenever Tori arrived, Mrs. Blair would be busy preparing a meal or tidying the family room, but she was always interested in hearing about her day. She was only a few inches taller than Tori, and had a full face that was usually framed by wisps of hair that fell from a loose bun. Over the years, little creases had formed at the corners of her eyes. Tori thought it was probably from so much smiling. Mrs. Blair had known her since she was born and was like part of the family. The girls followed Tori through the garage door, kicked off their shoes and hurried into the kitchen.

"Hi, Mrs. B.," called Tori.

"Hello, Tori…girls," Mrs. Blair replied. She looked over the disheveled girls streaked with blue, and her gaze landed on Tori's stained face. "Hmm, something tells me you didn't come straight home from school today. Perhaps you want to wash up first, and I'll fix you a snack."

Suddenly the girls burst into a recount of the afternoon's activities.

"You won't believe what happened!" Tori exclaimed.

"It was so scary!" said Angie.

"The boys are so mean," said Kelly.

"Okay, one at a time," Mrs. Blair calmly advised.

Angie stepped forward, her brown eyes flashing with excitement as she began to tell the story. She felt at home at Tori's house because the two girls had lived close by since the neighborhood was built six years ago. "We heard that the boys were staying after school today because their soccer team was in the playoffs."

"Yeah," chimed in Kelly. "It would have been the perfect chance to reclaim our clubhouse."

Kelly Norton had moved to Coreyville just two years ago, and quickly became friends with her classmates. She lived in a neighborhood within walking distance of Angie and Tori. The three were inseparable. Kelly had straight hair that matched her brown eyes, which were framed by trendy glasses. For someone who loved to shop and dress in the latest styles, she looked out of character with her hair in disarray. Her eyes lit up as she rapidly related the story. "We even had a new lock to keep the boys out."

"My brother got a new bike lock and gave me his old one," continued Angie. "Everything was perfect. We ran all the way to the path through the woods, and just when we thought it was safe, the enemy appeared!"

"It turns out, the other soccer team didn't have enough players, and the game was cancelled!" explained Tori.

"They had blueberries!" continued Angie.

"So I see," said Mrs. Blair, studying the girls' faces and clothes. "You have had quite a day." She set out cups of juice and graham crackers. "Now clean up and try to calm down before you have your snack."

The girls crowded around the kitchen sink and started sudsing up their hands.

"Okay, let's get started planning our next raid," said Kelly.

"Maybe we should sneak in before school next time," suggested Tori.

"Or Sunday, after church. They would never

expect that," offered Angie.

Kelly and Tori nodded in agreement as each pulled up a stool to the counter, grabbed a graham cracker and noisily ate as they continued talking about their plans.

"I don't mean to be putting my nose into your business," said Mrs. Blair. "But don't you think if you put your minds to it you could come up with a better solution?"

"Gee, Mrs. B," Angie began to explain, "the girls and boys have been fighting over this clubhouse for years. We have to win it back."

"I understand. It's just sometimes it doesn't hurt to think of alternatives. Why don't you finish up your snacks and get ready to head home? You can get together tomorrow or over the weekend if you want, but Tori's dad is coming home soon, I've got to get dinner ready and, judging from your backpacks, you all have homework to do."

"That's for sure," said Kelly. "Thanks for the snack, Mrs. B."

"Let's get together on Saturday and make our plan," said Angie.

"Let's do it Sunday," said Tori. "My dad has some work thing I have to go to with him on Saturday."

"Okay, call me Saturday night," said Angie.

"Me, too," said Kelly.

They all waved goodbye. Tori cleared up the snacks with Mrs. Blair, grabbed her backpack and headed to her room to do her homework.

3

"Ten minutes, Tori!" Mr. Conroy called from the landing at the bottom of the steps.

"I'll be right down!" Tori called back. She looked for her favorite purple scrunchy but couldn't find it. Instead she chose a purple headband and carefully pulled her hair away from her face. She put a light coat of lip gloss on and inhaled the fragrance. *Mmm, cotton candy,* she thought as she closed her eyes for a second and enjoyed the scent.

Tori quickly went downstairs and found her dad staring into the hallway mirror, trying on ties.

"Which one?" he asked Tori as he posed with each tie in front of his shirt.

Tori wrinkled her nose at the first two he modeled, then nodded approval of a dark red tie with a diamond pattern.

"Red it is! Shall we go?" The two left the house and climbed into their dark green truck.

Today was the grand opening of the new Decker office building downtown, and Mr. Conroy was invited because his company was in charge of designing the inside office space and purchasing office furniture for the building. It was located in downtown Pittsburgh, and they reached the main gate of the headquarters in about thirty-five minutes. Her father stopped the truck at the security booth and showed his invitation to a uniformed man who waved his arm, indicating the direction they should continue. Now the impressive building was in full view. Tori looked up in amazement.

There is so much glass, she thought to herself.

"There is so much glass," her father said.

Tori smiled, happy to know that an adult was just as much in awe of the grand structure. The two got out of the car, and Mr. Conroy took her hand as they walked in through the huge revolving glass doors.

Tori felt proud and a little grown-up to be attending the opening with her dad. She had been going to events with him throughout her childhood and felt comfortable around adults. She wore a long black skirt with flat black boots and a soft sweater that was purple, her favorite color.

Her dad was tall with short brown hair that was just starting to grey, and since turning forty-six, he would now say he was in his "mid-forties." In college he was a basketball player and still played in a church league. In the spring, he and Angie's dad coached the girls' basketball team.

As they entered the building, they were greeted with lively music from a trio of musicians sitting on a small platform to their left. Tori could identify a cello, a violin and a flute, instruments she had learned about in music class. She and her dad immediately turned their attention upward to take in the view of a huge open atrium. It enabled them to see the ceiling that had so much glass, she felt like she was still outdoors. Each of the eight floors opened onto the atrium, and each had a walkway wrapping around the outer edge with a railing so people could look down on the center from any floor.

The entrance was filled with people, and the second floor had people lined up around the railing looking down on the activities. In the center of the room was an elegant fountain. A small stage had been built for the event, skirted in royal blue cloth. On it were six chairs, a podium, microphone and an American flag. About one hundred chairs were set up in rows facing the stage.

A man dressed in a dark suit and tie walked up the four steps to the stage and turned on the microphone, tapping it twice to check if it was on. The microphone made an annoying, loud squawking sound that caught the attention of the guests. He motioned to the musicians to stop playing, and announced that the program was about to begin.

Tori moved toward the chairs, pulling her father by the hand, but the chairs filled up immediately.

"It's okay, Tori," said Mr. Conroy. "We can stand back here."

Tori shrugged her shoulders and agreed. She was used to it, because her dad often wanted to be able to leave quickly from this type of event.

Looking over the sea of people, she searched for a familiar face, but found none. She spotted two other children that looked to be her age, but didn't recognize them.

The mayor was introduced, and she listened intently as he welcomed the people who would work in the new offices to the community.

The revolving glass doors swooshed, and a woman slipped in behind the Conroys.

"Excuse me," she whispered to Mr. Conroy. "Am I late?"

Mr. Conroy turned and looked down at the woman.

"I beg your pardon," he said.

"Have I missed anything?"

"No, they just got started and are about to introduce the man who built it."

"Oh," the woman responded. "Good, then I guess I'm just in time."

"I guess so," Mr. Conroy continued, "if you like this kind of thing."

"I suppose these speeches can get rather boring," the woman agreed pleasantly.

"You've heard one, you've heard them all. But I do have to say, this building is outstanding, and this guy who runs Alvarez Construction certainly knows what he is doing."

"Really?" she replied. "Do you think he does?"

"You can bet on it. From what I've seen, he's probably one of the best in the business."

The woman smiled and nodded her head.

"By the way, I'm Bob Conroy." He turned and extended his hand.

"Nice to meet you, Bob," replied the woman as they shook hands. "I'm Lucinda."

"And this is my daughter, Tori," added Mr. Conroy.

Tori and the woman shook hands and smiled. Tori turned her attention back to the mayor's speech.

"Well, Lucinda, here comes the big speaker introduction," said Mr. Conroy.

The mayor began, "Alvarez Construction is a

Construction Management, Commercial General Contractor, Development and Design/Build Firm that has successfully built stadiums, entertainment facilities, convention centers and exhibit halls, industrial, educational, government, housing and office projects throughout the United States and in Latin America.

"The owner and president is a nationally recognized speaker and advocate for business issues. Please join me in welcoming the President of Alvarez Construction, Lucinda Catalina Alvarez."

"Excuse me," whispered the woman to Mr. Conroy, "I've got to go up to the podium for a moment. Why don't you and Tori join me as my guests at the head table afterward for the luncheon?" she said as she slipped past.

Mr. Conroy stood with his mouth open as he realized what a huge mistake he had made. He incorrectly assumed the owner of the construction company was a man. The color rose in his cheeks.

"Good job, Dad," Tori teased.

"It was just a simple mistake. Anyone could have made it," he responded sheepishly.

"I don't think so," she playfully scolded.

"Maybe we should just slip out the door while no one is watching," suggested Mr. Conroy.

"Shhh, you aren't listening to Ms. Alvarez," whispered Tori. "Besides, I heard her invite us to lunch."

Mr. Conroy let out a loud sigh, and the two stayed through the end of the program.

4

"Buildings create functional environments for government, hospitals, offices, churches, homes, restaurants and retail stores," Ms. Alvarez said, as she continued her speech. "Nothing happens without buildings. These structures influence how people work and live. Over the centuries, they enabled civilization to thrive. You can get an idea of how people lived centuries ago when you look at the bridges, cathedrals and towers that were built in Europe during those years.

"People spend so much of their time at the workplace that we wanted to make sure the Decker building would provide a comfortable, practical and lovely space that fit well into the community. Thank you to all of my team who worked tirelessly over the past two years, and welcome to the many people who will call the Decker building their home-away-from-home while they are at work."

Applause sprang up from the crowd, and Ms. Alvarez smiled in return. The man with the dark suit rose from his chair to finish the program.

"There is one more thing I would like to say, if I may," Ms. Alvarez interjected. "I am happy to say that I work with a wonderful group of people. But I think it's important to note that more than half of that team are women.

"You see, when I grew up, girls wore only dresses to school. My mother helped me believe that it would not always be that way, but it was hard to understand, because I wanted to run track, jump hurdles and compete in athletics in elementary school, which was not permitted for girls then.

"My older brothers, all five of them, played a lot of sports, and I grew up feeling comfortable in non-traditional environments for girls and young women. When I was in fifth grade, I asked to compete in the high jump event at my school's annual Sports Day, and was told that girls didn't do that type of thing. My parents supported my desire to participate and my mother talked to the principal. While he was absolutely not in favor of the idea, eventually he agreed to allow me to compete that year. I was the only girl, the shortest and by far the skinniest. But I won.

"To my surprise, my winning was received with mixed attitudes. On one hand, many were excited that the field was now opening for other girls. On the other hand, many thought a girl shouldn't be

18

doing such a thing. All I know is that it gave me great satisfaction knowing I had enabled other girls to become more involved in competitive athletics.

"I use many of the skills and values I gained from that experience in my business today, such as developing strategy, working with a team and taking risks. So when you leave today and see the plaque hanging at the entrance door, you will notice that there are not just my initials on it, but my full name, because I want people to know that a woman constructed this building."

An outburst of applause filled the room as the audience rose to their feet. Tori beamed at her dad and clapped until her hands hurt.

The man in the dark suit shook Ms. Alvarez's hand and moved close to the microphone. "Thank you, Ms. Alvarez, and thank you all for coming this afternoon and welcoming us to the community," he said. "Please join us in our company cafeteria for a luncheon."

"That's us!" Tori said, smiling sweetly at her dad. She grabbed his hand and lead him toward the large crowd that was moving under the archway leading to the cafeteria.

Tori spotted Ms. Alvarez at the head table motioning to join her, and they quickly made their way through the crowd.

"That was a great speech, Ms. Alvarez!" said Tori. "You are a terrific speaker and an awesome builder!"

"Thank you, Tori," said Ms. Alvarez. "I'll let you in on a little secret. I still get nervous talking in front of crowds."

Tori smiled in agreement.

"Hello, Lucinda," Mr. Conroy greeted Ms. Alvarez. "I owe you a big apology."

"Apology accepted," she replied. "That was not the first time someone expected me to be a man."

"The new office headquarters is magnificent. You must be very proud."

"I am. I have a terrific team to thank for that."

A bell rang out, signaling the meal was about to be served. Ms. Alvarez motioned for the Conroys to sit, and she made introductions around the table.

Tori was amazed by the perfectly set table. She remembered her aunt's wedding that was almost as beautiful. There were three forks, two spoons and a knife at her setting. She felt sophisticated and confused at the same time. She watched the others to see what utensil they picked up first.

"Outside to inside," Ms. Alvarez whispered.

"Excuse me?" Tori questioned.

"Use the outside utensil first."

Tori stared at her silverware as she finally understood. "Oh, I get it!" she laughed, picking up the fork on the outside and starting to eat her salad.

"So, Tori, what grade are you in?" asked Ms. Alvarez.

"Fifth grade," she replied. "I start middle school next year."

"That's quite a big change. You must be very excited."

"I am," she said as she took another bite.

"Do you live close to the city?"

"Just about 30 minutes away in Coreyville," replied Mr. Conroy.

"Oh, my family was from there!" said Ms. Alvarez. "My mother and father retired to Florida about 15 years ago, and I moved into the city. I haven't been back except for a high school reunion about eight years ago. I went to Shamona Elementary School."

"Wow! That's my school," said Tori.

"Boy, does that bring back memories," said Ms. Alvarez. "I remember how I loved my third grade teacher, Miss Elvin."

"She is Mrs. Tomlinson now and Vice Principal of the school," said Mr. Conroy.

"I also remember how I loved playing in the band," she recalled.

"Really?" asked Tori. "What did you play?"

"The clarinet. Do you play an instrument?"

"The piano," she replied. "But I'm not in the band. I'm in chorus. It's a lot of fun."

"Another thing I remember," Ms. Alvarez said as she shook her head back and forth slowly, "it seems so funny now...the boys and the girls had a huge rivalry over an old fort in the woods."

"What kind of fort?" asked Tori.

"Well, it was an old wooden shack right along the path from the school to one of the neighborhoods," she replied. "We used to call it the tin can since it had an old tin roof."

"No way!" Tori exclaimed. "It's still there!"

"You're kidding!" said Ms. Alvarez.

"No, it's really there, but the boys took it over last fall."

"Well, that won't do."

"I know, but we don't know what to do about it," said Tori. "Last fall, the girls were in control of the clubhouse – that's what we call it now. We had it during the whole summer. We had meetings on Saturday mornings and Wednesdays after school. We told stories, sang songs, played games...it was so much fun.

"Then, in October, Max's big brother came home to visit from college, and that's when they came up with a plan that ruined our fun. The Friday night before Halloween, someone came in and took down our curtains, put all our stuff outside and put a lock on the door. We found it like that Saturday morning. We thought it must have been the boys but didn't know for sure until Halloween. Then we saw three of the boys wearing our curtains tied up like bandannas as part of their costumes!"

Ms. Alvarez and Mr. Conroy tried not to laugh at the thought of the boys wearing the curtains around their heads.

"And that's the last time we've been in the clubhouse," continued Tori. "We've tried all kinds of ways to get it back, but they are always ready for us."

"That's a shame," said Ms. Alvarez.

"Kids," said Mr. Conroy.

Tori gave her dad a look. "You don't understand," she said with a pout.

"Oh, honey, I understand more than you know," he said. "That clubhouse was around when I was in school. It just seems a little silly now, that's all. Ms. Alvarez and I are grown up. Remember, Tori, Ms. Alvarez runs a big company, and there are more important things on our minds. I'm sure you understand."

"Yes," said Tori reluctantly. "I guess so." The disappointment showed on her face and there was an uncomfortable silence at the table.

"Well," Ms. Alvarez started slowly. "Actually, I think this is very important."

"You do?" asked Tori.

"You do?" echoed her father.

"Sure. I remember how exciting it was to have our very own place where we could get together and make plans and have fun. And I remember how disappointing it was to have it all taken away."

"But what can we do about it?" Tori asked.

"Well…what do you think you can do?" Ms. Alvarez asked.

"I guess what we've always done," she replied. "Wait for a chance when we can take it over again, but this time, get a better lock."

"Okay, that's an option," Ms. Alvarez paused and then continued, "then what would happen?"

"I guess the boys would just get it back again sooner or later," said Tori.

"So, any other ideas?"

Tori started to feel uncomfortable as she searched her mind for alternatives. "Not really," she finally admitted, "unless we built our own."

Ms. Alvarez did not answer, but simply smiled at Tori across the table. Tori's eyes grew wide. "Do you think we could really build one?"

Mr. Conroy raised his eyebrows, finding it hard to believe that Ms. Alvarez would encourage the

25

girls to build a clubhouse.

"It would certainly take some time, and you would have to get the materials, but if you can get the people to help build it, I'll help you plan it," she said.

"Really?"

"Really?" her father echoed.

"Really," replied Ms. Alvarez.

"Dad?" She looked at her dad pleadingly.

He nodded his approval.

"Terrific! Now if you will both excuse me," said Ms. Alvarez, "I must visit with my client before the end of the afternoon. Tori, here is my business card."

The card read:

> Lucinda Catalina Alvarez
> President and Chief Executive Officer
> Alvarez Construction

"Why don't you call my assistant on Monday. She will schedule an appointment next week so I can help you get your plans off the ground."

Ms. Alvarez extended her hand and they shook.

"You've got a deal!" announced Tori.

5

Tori couldn't wait to call Angie and Kelly to tell them about her encounter. The moment she got home, she raced to the phone in the den. They decided to meet Monday afternoon.

~ ~ ~

As soon as school was over, they hurried to Tori's house and called Ms. Alvarez's office to schedule an appointment as she instructed.

"Thursday at 4:30," announced Tori as she placed the handset on the cradle.

"Here we go!" Angie said as she raised a juice box in the air.

Kelly and Tori raised theirs to make a toast.

"To our clubhouse!" Angie said.

"To our clubhouse!" they replied in unison.

6

On Thursday afternoon, Angie's mom, Mrs. Donovan, picked the girls up from school. They put their backpacks in the rear of the van and sat on the back bench seat, three across. Mrs. Donovan suggested they ride the train to avoid traffic driving into Pittsburgh. The 30-minute ride would take them to a station just a few minutes from Ms. Alvarez's building.

They watched through the windows as the towns went flashing by. They could see people in their backyards gardening, kids walking home from school and truck drivers delivering supplies to local stores. The view changed from winding roads and yards with trees, fences and swing sets to small shops, lots of street lights and cars parked on the side of the road, then finally to skyscrapers, with pavement and parking lots replacing the trees. Soon the Pittsburgh skyline was in view.

Suddenly the train grew dark and the sound of the train on the tracks was very loud as it went through a tunnel. The girls giggled with surprise and excitement. The train jolted to a stop as it pulled into the underground terminal. It was 4:10. They had twenty minutes to spare.

As they came out of the terminal, the sunshine caused them to squint. The aroma of hot chestnuts filled the air as they passed a street vendor who was selling snacks from a cart. They walked two blocks, checking out the department store windows and looking upward at the tall buildings, while Mrs. Donovan constantly reminded them to watch for traffic and look where they were going.

Ms. Alvarez had offices on the twenty-fourth floor of a skyscraper on Grant Street. Her assistant greeted them and offered to take their coats, then let Ms. Alvarez know that her "4:30" had arrived.

Tori led the way into Ms. Alvarez's office. It was beautiful and busy. Facing the door was an antique wooden desk with a large picture window behind it that offered an amazing view of the city. There were three comfortable chairs and a sofa, just like a living room, and a large, flat table that had paper in big rolls and large blueprints spread across it.

"Tori, welcome!" Ms. Alvarez stood up from her chair and greeted her guests.

Tori introduced her friends and Mrs. Donovan to Ms. Alvarez.

"Have a seat," their hostess said, as she gestured

for them all to sit down.

Tori sank into one of the plush chairs. Her mind raced as she tried to take in all she saw in the room. Shelves on one wall were lined with pottery, books, photographs and a little frame that displayed a ribbon with a medal. Tori thought it must be the one Ms. Alvarez won when she was a child.

"So you are going to build a clubhouse," Tori suddenly came back to the moment as she heard Ms. Alvarez's voice.

The girls nodded with enthusiasm.

"Well, the first thing I do with my clients is discuss what part the structure will play in people's lives," said Ms. Alvarez. "For instance, will it be an environment where people go to learn, like a school – or work, like an office building – or perhaps gather, like a church?"

"Well, I can answer the first question," offered Angie. "This will be a place for girls to have fun."

"It's a place where we want to spend time together and make plans, talk and play," added Kelly.

"Good," Ms. Alvarez encouraged the girls. "Next, we look at the atmosphere, or the feeling we want to create. Should it be cozy, exciting, peaceful or businesslike?"

"Definitely cozy," said Tori.

"And colorful," added Angie.

"Okay, now we are making progress," said Ms. Alvarez. "We will have to determine how big it needs to be and how it fits into the community."

"They can build it in the field behind our yard, as long as it's not an eyesore," said Mrs. Donovan.

"What's an izor?" questioned Kelly.

"Not 'izor'!" Angie replied as she rolled her eyes. "Eyesore. You know, like a big mess."

"Oh. Right. I knew that," said Kelly sheepishly. "It won't be an eyesore."

"I'm sure that won't be a problem," answered Ms. Alvarez with a laugh. "Of course, another point we have to discuss is what kind of budget we have to work with."

At that the girls squirmed and made faces.

"We really don't have much of a budget," said Angie.

"Well, I didn't expect that you would," replied Ms. Alvarez. "But I think there will be ways to get around that. I know you girls are willing to work hard, and Tori, your dad said he would be happy to help supply some of the lumber and supervise the construction. But you will have to take some time and calculate how much you have available to spend and then stay within that budget."

"We know we have a lot of work ahead of us,"

31

Tori said.

"And we are all willing to do what it takes," Angie continued enthusiastically.

After a short silence, Kelly noticed all eyes were on her. "Right! Absolutely! Ready to work," she agreed.

"Okay, girls, that's the spirit!" Ms. Alvarez concluded. "Well, the conversation we just had is actually very similar to the kind of discussions I have with many of my clients, even those who are planning a large skyscraper, school or hotel.

"Our company becomes a partner in the design and development of each project we take on. Sometimes we handle every aspect of the project, from the planning and design, to the actual construction. In other cases, we might work with an outside architectural firm to determine the design. We are very flexible so we can work with each client in the manner that works best. Why don't we take a tour of the offices, and I'll explain to you the different aspects of our construction company?"

With that, Mrs. Donovan and the girls eagerly followed Ms. Alvarez into the hallway, where she motioned to her right and pointed out an office behind a large glass wall that revealed five people at a long, smooth wooden conference table covered with blueprints, pens, coffee mugs, water bottles, laptop computers and a plate of cookies. Large whiteboards bearing scribbled lists surrounded them on two walls. One person stood at a board, talking enthusiastically and waving a blue marker.

"Here is an actual example of the first phase of a construction project," said Ms. Alvarez. "This is what we call the *pre-construction phase*, where we sit down with our clients and create a detailed design. The design has to suit the needs of our client's vision, various uses and budget. We look at every aspect, very much like we just discussed for yours. We talk about the size of the project, function, colors, the environment the client hopes to create, any constraints or challenges we will face, types of building materials, such as wood or brick, even to the details of what kind of wood or brick."

"This part must be so much fun, because you can really use your imaginations," Tori concluded enthusiastically.

"On one hand you are right," Ms. Alvarez agreed. "However, you have to keep in mind that you need permission from the appropriate local officials to build your structure where and how you want to build it. Only specific types of buildings may be constructed in certain areas, and the officials are careful to ensure these rules are followed.

"Even though your project is small, you need permission from your families, and you should check with your township officials as well."

The friends exchanged worried glances.

"I'm sure you will not have a problem. I just wanted to illustrate the importance of getting permission."

"Gee, I guess it never ends," said Kelly. "Even when you're a grown-up."

"Let's move down the hall a little and take a look at our *design and architectural team*." The girls crowded into the doorway and looked into a large room divided into a few cubicles and a spacious area with large tables, some with machines and some with large flat pages stacked on them.

"Here is where we create computer renderings of the actual plans. You would be amazed how important math and computer skills are during this phase. Let's take a look at what MaryBeth is working on."

The girls gathered around a young woman working at a computer.

"Wow! It looks like virtual reality!" Kelly exclaimed with delight.

"So much of the design phase has been enhanced by the use of computers. We now have the ability to use three-dimensional computerized visualization. It's amazing how far we've come and how computers have enabled us to do much more, much faster. So my advice to you girls is to keep your computer skills sharp!"

"Things have certainly changed since I got my first job," Mrs. Donovan was shaking her head as she watched in awe.

"Our designers take the computer drawings and enlarge them on these printers," Ms. Alvarez continued. "Then we lay tissue paper over the drawing so the original floor plan is still visible under the tissue. That makes it easier for us to make notes or changes, or compare alternative ideas without touching the original plan. Sometimes we have to go 'back to the drawing board' and try a different approach. Once we get a building plan that the client approves, we determine the estimated costs of the plan. Of course, the design was developed to fit a specific budget, but now we look at all the details and how much they will cost. Let's move on and I'll explain."

They all followed Ms. Alvarez from the room and down the hall. "This is a very important function of our design and architectural team. It's what we call *estimating* and *value engineering.*"

"My brother is studying engineering at college," Kelly chimed in.

"That's excellent," said Ms. Alvarez. "You may

be interested in following his footsteps if you like architecture, design or construction. At this point, our value engineering team begins an even more detailed review, analyzing the proposed materials and products specified, the cost of all the building components, the time required for manufacture and delivery, and the amount of labor needed for installation.

"The team also reviews the electrical, plumbing, mechanical and security systems to determine not just the cost, but the functionality and durability that different types of systems could provide. For example, the roof design may be one that is less expensive based on the roofing material or amount of labor needed to install, but such a roof will last for a relatively short time. Our team might recommend another type of roof that costs more at the beginning, but lasts much longer before needing repair or replacement. This gives the owner a choice when making budget decisions.

"The engineers evaluate every major aspect of the structure. Should the building be rasied off the ground? Will it have good drainage to be protected from rain flow? What type and how many stairways, elevators, entrances and exits will be required?

"In your case, perhaps you will want to look

at details such as what kind of flooring you can afford, how you will protect your clubhouse from the boys, and even how you can differentiate it from theirs."

"I get it!" said Tori. "Like, maybe we will have a fence around ours."

"Or a really strong door," added Angie.

"And we can paint a mural on the outside so it looks really cool," Kelly suggested.

"Exactly," Ms. Alvarez encouraged the girls. "You will have the clubhouse of envy!"

This met with a round of smiles and giggles as she continued. "You obviously understand the idea of value engineering, and you probably realize how important this phase is because it helps you become very realistic about your design and the associated costs. Can you afford the fence, the door or even a mural?"

With that comment, the girls were quiet, as they knew they had a very meager budget. "I can see you are starting to get the idea of how difficult the construction process can be. Our *estimating department* puts together cost models and obtains pricing for our clients so they can determine how they can pay for the project and make necessary changes."

They followed Ms. Alvarez down a flight of steps in silence, admiring six large framed photos of projects that had been completed by the company. There was a school, two high-rise buildings, a church, a 37-story hotel and a grocery store.

"How do you know how to create so many different types of buildings?" asked Kelly.

"That's the beauty of this business," Ms. Alvarez answered. "Every project is different...with a different function, size, budget and environment. Yet we approach each project in a similar manner by determining what the client envisions and what resources are available. Then the challenge comes in using our creativity and expertise to develop it using our resources wisely. The pride at the completion of the project is part of what makes all the hard work worth it."

"I don't know how you can keep track of all the different jobs and people," Angie commented.

"That's a good point, Angie. There *are* a lot of steps in the process. It's important to plan all the building activities in the right order," Ms. Alvarez explained. "For instance, you can't schedule a day to paint if you haven't first finished sanding and preparing the walls. And before you do that, you have to put up the drywall. That's where our *scheduling department* comes in. Those people develop a plan detailing how we put all the steps of the project together, how long each step will take, and who is responsible.

"Even with the best planning, you have to allow for the unexpected, like rain, a worker getting sick, a late delivery…the list goes on. So we plan time for those types of delays. You will need to write down every job, determine how many hours or days each will take and schedule who will accomplish it. You also need to make a list of all the supplies you will require, and when they must be delivered to the building site. Remember, there isn't much storage space, so you'll have to figure out how to protect everything from the weather or getting 'lost.'

"Here's an example of how we plan a job with a flow chart," she said, pointing to a large chart hanging on the wall in the office at which they had arrived. Across the top was a row indicating days of the week, and along the left hand side was a column of activities. Round colored magnets were positioned along the chart to show which day a particular activity was to be accomplished. "The colors indicate which person or company is responsible for the day's activities."

"I love organizing things, like making calendars and lists," said Kelly enthusiastically. "I never thought I would fit into construction, but this is perfect for me!"

"It *is* perfect," said Angie, "'cause I sure don't

want to make the list."

"Of course, someone also has to be in charge of keeping people committed to the schedule," Ms. Alvarez added. "Otherwise it's meaningless."

"Now *that's* something I could do!" Angie stated.

"I think you will each find an area of construction that you will enjoy and excel at," said Ms. Alvarez. "Now, last, but certainly not least, is the actual *construction* portion of the project. All of the other activities happen first, leading up to the physical construction of the building. We manage the construction work by scheduling and coordinating all of the activities, which include the layout of the foundation, measuring where windows will be cut and installed, pouring concrete, carpentry, electrical work, plumbing and so on.

"Our company has *project managers* who work in the office and *construction superintendents* who work at the site to supervise activities. Safety and quality control are very important aspects of construction and we perform many inspections throughout the process, and of course everyone on the site wears hard hats."

"Cool!" Tori and Angie chimed together.

"Yuck!" Kelly gasped.

"Well, construction isn't always a glamorous

job," Ms. Alvarez smiled as she explained. "I can't say my hair always looks great, but I can tell you that the buildings we construct are all beautiful, no matter what their purpose. It's a wonderful feeling to know you are contributing to the environment of a community with a structure that might shelter people, house a business, or provide a place of learning for students. It's very creative and satisfying work."

Mrs. Donovan and the girls followed her up the stairs, which took them back to her office.

"Wow, that was fantastic," said Tori.

"I'm glad you enjoyed the tour," replied Ms. Alvarez. "I think you have a pretty good idea of what you have to do to plan your clubhouse. Now the ball is in your court. You have a lot of homework to do. Do you think you are up for the task?"

The girls nodded their heads in unison. "We are," Kelly spoke for all three.

With that, they committed to prepare a scheduling flow chart, material list, budget and sketch and send them to Ms. Alvarez within two weeks. Then they said their goodbyes and made their way back to the train station.

They arrived just in time to catch the six o'clock train home. It was crowded with commuters who traveled back and forth to their jobs every day from outside the city. They sat in silence, and the motion of the train and constant sound of the wheels clicking on the track made Tori feel drowsy. As her mind wandered, she realized this was going to be a big project...maybe more than they could handle.

7

For the next two weeks, the girls were constantly on the phone, e-mailing and at each other's houses, planning, talking and drawing out their ideas for their clubhouse. In school, Tori doodled different floor plans in her math notebook. Angie sketched how she wanted the outside to look and Kelly prepared lists of materials they would need along with the associated costs.

Their dream was starting to take shape. Since Kelly was eager to help organize the project and Tori was handy with a computer, they worked together to prepare a schedule that listed the particular task, who was responsible and when it was due.

The girls met Saturday mornings after soccer and Wednesday afternoons to go over their plans and task list. On the second Saturday, they decided to meet at Angie's house. They tossed their cleats in a pile in the garage and went down to the basement, where they pulled out their sketches and lists so they could come up with a final plan. Angie set out a large art pad, a ruler and pencil, and prepared to draw the plan.

"We definitely need room for a large table in the middle," began Tori.

Angie drew an area representing a 10-foot by 10-foot space and sketched a table in the middle.

"Yeah, but if we want to move around and dance, we are going to need open space for that," said Kelly.

With a quick erasure of a line, Angie enlarged the space to 12-foot by 14-foot.

"I want to have a closet so we can keep some games and stuff handy," added Tori.

"We could keep some snacks there, too," agreed Kelly.

Angie erased the outside line again and added two feet to the depth of the clubhouse.

"Don't you think we will want to have a party once in a while?" asked Kelly.

The girls looked questioningly at each other and there was a silent pause.

Angie nodded and erased the borders once more to add 3 feet to either side.

"It would be cool to sleep over, maybe we could put in a few cots so we don't have to sleep on the ground," suggested Tori.

"That would be cool," agreed Kelly.

"Cots," Angie repeated and enlarged the perimeter 3 feet on all sides.

"Do you think we need a little entranceway where we can hang up our coats and stuff?" asked Kelly.

"Okay, look, guys," Angie finally spoke up. "I'm just about out of paper here. So far we have a 20-foot by 20-foot clubhouse. I doubt we have enough money to build one even half that size."

"Whoops," Tori grinned sheepishly.

"I guess we got carried away a little," added Kelly.

"We?" Angie replied.

"Okay, so maybe we don't need the coat area," Tori offered.

"Or, um, the cots," added Kelly.

"I think we better sleep on this and try again on Wednesday," suggested Angie.

"Agreed!" said Tori.

"Who wants ice cream?" asked Angie. With that, they dropped their plans and raced up the stairs.

8

By Wednesday at 5:00 pm the girls had finalized their plan. They decided on a more modest 12-foot by 12-foot structure with two windows, a door and a floor. They would use plywood that Tori's father would supply. Each of the girls was contributing $25 to purchase drywall for the walls.

Angie's parents donated the paint. That meant they would have to abandon their hope of a colorful interior and settle for the same pale green as Angie's dining room, but they were thankful to get the donation. They still had to find a way to cover the roof and buy the windows and the door. Still, they were on their way. They e-mailed Ms. Alvarez with their plans:

> Dear Ms. Alvarez,
> Thank you for helping us plan our clubhouse. We decided what kind of environment we want and what budget we have available. Then, we prepared a plan (Kelly's brother let us use his software). We

put together a scheduling flow chart, assigned responsibilities and due dates. And we also listed our supplies and estimated the costs for them. Although we went $14 over our budget, we think we can convince our parents to help us if we keep good grades and really work hard! We attached the lists and a scan of our plan. We are very excited and can't wait to get started. Please let us know what you think. Thank you again for all of your help and encouragement.

Your friends,
Tori, Angie and Kelly

CLUBHOUSE PLAN

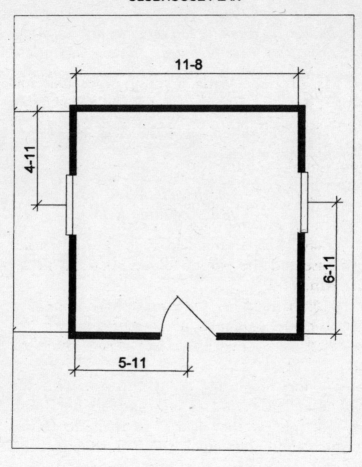

9

"Ms. Alvarez," Maria, a young office assistant, caught her boss' attention just as she was packing up to leave the office on Wednesday evening. "I hate to bother you on your way out, but I thought you would be interested in the e-mail that just came in."

"Can it wait until tomorrow?"

"I think you will want to see it."

"Okay," Ms. Alvarez said as she put down her briefcase and the pile of folders she held under her arm.

Maria handed her the e-mail she had printed out from her computer just minutes before. She watched as a smile broke out across her boss' face.

"So, they are really going through with the clubhouse!" she said as she nodded her head. "Good! I knew they had it in them to follow through, and they stuck to their timeline and got this to me when they said they would. Now wouldn't it be nice if all of our clients were this punctual?"

~ ~ ~

The next day Ms. Alvarez reviewed the plans, made some notes and suggestions and e-mailed them back. After a week of communicating back and forth, the girls had a solid design.

All through the holiday season, they had fun perfecting their ideas. Tori visited her mother during the break, and when she returned, the girls started collecting materials and determined how much more money they would have to raise. The cold Pittsburgh winter made it impossible to start their project until the ground softened. They decided they would start building outside the first week in April, but it seemed like forever.

10

"Are you awake?" Tori whispered to Angie. Angie didn't flinch.

"Are you awake?" Tori questioned Kelly in the same hushed tone. Kelly was still for a few seconds, then suddenly grabbed the edge of her sleeping bag and squirmed deeper into the fluffy folds.

With a gentle probe of her index finger, Tori nudged Angie's head. "Are you awake?"

"I'm awake. Okay?" Angie replied in a sleepy monotone that implied, *go away.*

Waiting for the girls to wake up was torture for Tori. April had arrived. This morning they would begin construction of the clubhouse. They had been up late last night talking about their plans and she could hardly sleep. She woke before the alarm, and laid in her sleeping bag for as long as she could before she simply had to wake the others.

"Okay, great! Let's go! Last one to the kitchen is a rotten egg," she called out as she ran up the basement stairs to the kitchen. After about three

51

minutes, she returned to the top of the steps and called down with her best whining voice, "Come on, guys!"

First Angie appeared with tousled hair, wearing her robe inside out. Then Kelly made her way to the kitchen table and laid her head on her crossed arms.

"What you girls need is a good breakfast," announced Tori. She produced a carton of eggs, butter and a pan, and proceeded to scramble eggs. They seemed to do the trick. As their stomachs got fuller, the conversation got livelier, and by nine o'clock, they had finished eating, gotten dressed and were ready to get to work.

They walked over to Angie's house where the supplies had been delivered that week. Angie's dog, Toby, greeted the girls with excited barks and escorted them to the backyard. The first job was the one they looked forward to least…digging the foundation.

Since the clubhouse wouldn't have a cement foundation like bigger structures, their job was to dig a shallow level area which would be filled with pebbles; then a simple wood floor and the walls of the clubhouse would be built on top. The process comprised digging deep holes at the four corners. With the help of their parents, they would position tall beams in each hole and pour wet concrete in to surround and stabilize them. The beams would serve as the skeleton. Once the concrete hardened, they would attach a long, horizontal beam at the base of each upright one, forming a rectangular wooden outline. Then they would carefully lay the floor planks across the beams, nailing them in place.

Each girl picked up a shovel and walked over to the area they had marked with rope on the ground to indicate the outline of the clubhouse.

Angie raised her shovel in preparation to make the first break in the earth.

"Wait!" Tori screamed.

"What?" Angie stopped and jumped away from the spot where she was about to dig. Kelly dropped her shovel and frantically looked at the ground as if a mouse might be lurking near her feet. Realizing they weren't in harm's way, they settled down and looked expectantly at Tori.

She looked sheepishly at them. "A picture," she said. "We need to take a picture. This is our groundbreaking!" She ran to her backpack and fished out her camera. At the same time, she called to Angie to ask her mom to come out and take their picture.

Mrs. Donovan arrived, still wearing her robe, carrying her camera and a video camera. "Okay, girls, grab some tools and stand over near the ropes," she directed them. The three friends stood in the center of the outlined area with their equipment.

"Smile!" Angie swung her drill up as if it were a lethal weapon. Kelly laughed and followed suit with her hammer and best secret-agent pose, and Tori displayed her hard hat proudly on top of her shovel. *Snap!* Construction was officially underway.

11

For the next three weekends, and a few evenings after school, the girls worked together. They dug the foundation, and learned to measure and saw the wood to prepare the pieces they would need for the frame.

One Wednesday after school, Angie and Tori were working on the frame, carefully attaching the long 2-inch by 4-inch by 8-foot pieces of wood that would support the structure.

"Tori, you aren't getting the nails in the right way," Angie corrected. "They should be flat against the wood, the way the guy at the home store showed us."

"It's close enough," Tori replied. "It's not even going to show."

"Well, it's important that we do it right."

"It's right, it's just not perfect, okay?"

"Fine," Angie ended the confrontation. "Where's Kelly, anyway? This is the second time she hasn't shown to help on a Wednesday."

"I don't know," Tori said with a shrug of her shoulders. "She said she was meeting up with some friends on the playground and would be right over."

"Well, if she spent half as much time helping as she did doing her nails, we'd be done by now," Angie said, shaking her head.

"Hi," Kelly said, standing behind Angie.

Angie spun around, surprised to see Kelly, realizing she had heard everything. "Sorry, Kelly," Angie said. "But really, you just aren't helping enough."

"Yes I am, you just want everything to be perfect, and you don't seem to think I can do anything right."

"That's not true," Angie protested.

"Kelly's right, Angie," Tori added. "You're making me nuts telling me how to do everything."

"Well, you're supposed to be in charge, Tori, but it sure doesn't seem like it," Angie said. "Someone has to be the boss."

"Oh, and now that's you?" challenged Tori.

"Well, it looks that way," answered Angie.

The three friends stared at each other in stunned silence. Finally, Tori spoke. "Let's take a break from working. I'm sure when the clubhouse is finished, we'll all look back at this and laugh."

"Don't you mean 'if' it gets finished?" Angie said sarcastically.

"Come on, Angie, give us a break," Kelly said.

"Let's clean up this stuff," said Tori.

"If you don't mind, I didn't take any of it out and I really have to get home," Kelly said. "My mom is taking me shopping at four-thirty, and it's already four o'clock. You understand. Call me, okay?"

Angie and Tori exchanged glances of annoyance and cleaned up in silence. They put the tools and equipment away in the garage and went their separate ways.

12

"Hey, sleepyhead," Mr. Conroy called in to Tori's room where she lay sleeping, face down, covers wound around her legs, her right arm dangling limply over the side of the bed.

"Hmmm," she groaned back.

"It's almost ten o'clock. How about getting your day started?"

"Hmmm."

"Don't you girls have a date to work on the clubhouse?" her dad inquired.

"No."

"What happened to 'we will get together every Saturday morning at nine o'clock to work?'"

"We're not."

"Okay, what's the matter?" He entered the room, cleared a place on the edge of her bed and sat down.

Tori rolled over, causing the sheets to tighten around her legs, and squirmed to free herself from the bonds of the huge knot of covers.

"This is a lot harder than I expected, Dad," she explained. "Angie is bossy and Kelly doesn't like to get dirty. No one is listening to me, and I feel like everything is getting messed up. We planned to finish by the end of school, and we only have two months left."

"Sounds like a problem," he agreed.

"That's for sure. No one is taking this seriously."

"It seems you have identified that Angie and Kelly aren't doing their parts," her father said.

"Exactly. I knew you'd understand."

"And what role are you playing?" Mr. Conroy asked.

"I'm the Project Manager."

"What is the Project Manager responsible for?"

"Ms. Alvarez said the Project Manager is supposed to coordinate all the work. She's in charge of keeping the project on schedule, on budget, seeing that the work gets done right and safely, and keeping the client satisfied."

"That's a big responsibility, and I'm going to guess that the Project Manager has to be skilled at solving problems," he suggested.

She let out a big sigh. "Are you blaming this whole mess on me?"

"No, Tori, I'm just suggesting that as Project Manager you realize that the others are looking to you to be a leader, and that good leadership can help solve a lot of problems."

"Like what, Dad? How can I get Kelly involved? She was great at the beginning when we were planning, and she was so enthusiastic."

"So can you help her use her strengths?"

"You mean like how she likes to organize things? Maybe if she made the work schedule instead of me, she would be better about following it."

"Exactly," Mr. Conroy smiled. "Being a leader doesn't mean taking over all the jobs."

"You know, Angie is so good at the actual building part, and I haven't listened to her at all. I should put her in charge of quality control."

"Good idea," he agreed.

"Okay, I think I get it."

"So, you'll consider getting out of bed?"

"Yes, I'm up and out!"

Tori slid into her slippers and shuffled her feet out the door, straight to the phone. She dialed Angie. "Angie, be at my house at noon, don't bring your hard hat, bring your bike. We are going to have some fun and take a new approach to this project!"

"Right on!" said Angie. "I'll call Kelly."

"Friends?" Tori asked.

"You bet!" said Angie.

61

13

Tori's new plan was working wonders. Kelly created weekly updates and calendars that helped the girls stay on track. She also kept shopping lists for supplies so they were sure to have the items they needed each week. Tori reviewed the plans to make sure they were staying on time and on budget. Angie reviewed the building plans and shared what she learned at the home store, along with some tips from her dad on the best ways to proceed.

Now that she realized it didn't mean she had to do everything herself, Tori liked her role as Project Manager. Sometimes their parents and families got involved, and they could see the results of their hard work. The structure started to resemble the clubhouse they had envisioned.

It was Sunday afternoon and the weather felt exactly as spring should. They sat with their backs against the trunk of a tall shade tree, enjoying its cool protection from the sun. Since the leaves were not yet full, the sun sneaked through, causing a polka dot effect on the girls' faces. They sipped from juice boxes and admired their work.

Plop! A cold blast of water burst from seemingly nowhere, splattering the girls and causing shrieks of surprise. They jumped to their feet as they tried quickly to determine what was happening. *Splat!* This time they saw it coming. A bright red water balloon flew from the woods, followed by muffled giggles. They knew exactly what was happening, and who was to blame.

"Max! We know it's you, Einstein and Ricky," Tori yelled to the bushes. "Come out and show your faces!"

The girls huddled and watched. Nothing happened.

"Cowards!" yelled Angie.

"You tell 'em, Angie," Kelly said as she inched behind her friend's body, waiting for the next airborne balloon.

Max appeared from behind the bushes, wearing a big grin, followed immediately by his crew of troublemakers, Ricky, Einstein and Ben.

As they walked over, the girls carefully looked for signs of balloons, blueberries or anything else that easily could be flung at them. Seeing no potential missiles, they came out from behind the protection of the tree to meet the boys.

"What's this?" asked Max as he looked over the clubhouse. "A doll house?"

"It's our clubhouse!" Kelly defended the structure.

"Doesn't look like a clubhouse," Ricky teased. "Looks like a hole with some sticks planted." That caused a short outbreak of laughter from the boys.

"Ignore them," Tori stated flatly to her friends. In her heart, it was hard to ignore. They had been working so hard, but they still had so much more work ahead of them. She wondered when they would ever actually get to use the clubhouse.

"Good luck," Max said. "Maybe by the time you graduate, there will be a roof on it. Come on guys, let's go to a real clubhouse." With that they headed back into the woods.

"We can't let them get away with this," said Angie.

"How can we just let them keep that clubhouse for themselves?" Kelly questioned.

"Come on, girls," Tori urged. "We're bigger than that. You know we are doing the right thing. When our clubhouse is finished, it will be wonderful and we will never have to put up with the boys again."

Little did the girls know that their troubles with the boys had only begun.

14

Monday afternoon, on the way home from school, the girls chatted about the day as they made their way toward the path that led through the woods.

"Don't look behind you," Tori cautioned Angie and Kelly. Both girls immediately glanced over their shoulders and spied Max, Ricky and Einstein.

"I said, 'don't look'," Tori scolded.

"Sorry, I couldn't help it," Kelly pleaded.

"Well, just act like we don't care," Tori said.

"Don't care about what?" Kelly inquired.

"Just be cool," Angie instructed.

"Right," Kelly agreed as she fixed her gaze straight ahead, tilted her head up a little and tossed her hair behind her shoulders.

Within minutes, the boys caught up to them and began speaking louder than necessary to assure they would be overheard.

"What do you say we get together to do our homework?" asked Max.

"Okay, where do you want to meet?" Ricky

asked.

"Hmmm, let's see, how about the clubhouse?" Max suggested.

"Yeah, the clubhouse," Einstein announced deliberately.

"It's great having a clubhouse, isn't it guys?" Max concluded.

"Excellent," agreed Ricky.

Tori rolled her eyes, Angie bit her lip and Kelly held her gaze forward while the boys passed them, but the taunting was almost more than they could stand.

"Someone hold me back," Angie held an eraser in her right hand, aimed carefully at Max's back.

"Angie!" Tori pleaded. "Remember what we said. We're bigger than that. Now, put the eraser down."

Angie hesitated, then reluctantly gave her friend the eraser and said, "But you have to admit, he deserved it." The girls grinned.

Suddenly, a thunderous noise filled the air.

"Wow! What was that?" Kelly asked. "Sounds like a stampede of elephants."

"I know, and it's coming from the woods," Tori agreed.

They picked up the pace and hurried down the path until they caught up to the boys, who had stopped at an orange plastic fence that prevented them from continuing on the path.

A man wearing a hard hat and a bright orange vest walked toward them and said, "Sorry kids, you can't walk through here."

"What's happening?" Max asked.

"Levine Construction is building a new neighborhood of 24 homes. We're going to be bulldozing the land and clearing trees and debris."

"But our clubhouse is in there," Max said.

"That's yours?" the man questioned. "We posted a notice on it twice that it's scheduled for demolition, but it doesn't look like anyone took it seriously."

The color rose in Max's face. "We thought the girls were playing a joke on us."

"This is no joke, boys. That shack will be gone in two days. If you want to come through with me, I'll escort you so you can take out anything valuable. But from now on, this area is off limits," he cautioned.

The girls listened in shocked silence. Einstein and Ricky stood stunned, unable to move, and Max could feel the sting of tears as he realized that their clubhouse would soon be gone.

15

The next day, the girls labored in silence, sharing a feeling of pride in their hard work. Their parents would join them later to finish the roof. That would leave only painting and some finishing touches. Nearing their deadline, they worked harder then ever to meet their goal.

Kelly created a database of names and addresses of people to invite to their dedication including their families, close friends, four teachers, the township manager, and, of course, Ms. Alvarez as the guest of honor.

Finally, Kelly broke the silence. "I can't believe the boys' clubhouse is gone."

Angie and Tori stopped what they were doing and put their tools down. "Oh my gosh, I know," Tori continued. "I actually feel bad for the boys."

"I feel worse for the clubhouse," said Angie. "Serves the boys right for being such creeps." She was surprised at the little pang of guilt she felt for thinking that way.

"I know you're right, but just think how we would feel," Kelly said.

"What do you think they are going to do about it?" Angie asked. "I can't picture them getting organized enough to build a new one, and summer is almost here."

"Guess they will have to live without one," Tori said.

"They are going to be awfully jealous of us," Kelly said.

"You know, you're right, Kelly," Tori said. "They will be very jealous."

"Very," Angie emphasized and exchanged glances with Tori.

"What?" Kelly questioned, feeling like she missed something.

"I have a plan," Tori announced with a sly smile.

16

The light from a full moon caused the trees to cast mysterious shadows. A light breeze caused the branches to sway gently back and forth, giving the eerie impression that the trees were whispering to each other. Saturday night was cool and a little damp. Occasionally a small creature would scurry through the underbrush.

Crack. The sound of a dead twig breaking filled the air.

"Shhh!" Max commanded.

"Sorry!" Ben whispered. "I didn't see it."

"Well, just be careful!"

"Okay!"

Einstein wondered why he let his little brother tag along. This was certainly a job for older boys. They had planned their attack carefully. If they weren't going to have a clubhouse, no one would. They had been waiting and watching patiently until the girls packed up their tools and left the yard, then, waited for nightfall. Armed with spray paint, toilet tissue and eggs, they had the perfect ingredients to ruin the girls' plans.

"Looks like the coast is clear," Max motioned to Ricky.

"Coast is clear," Ricky repeated to Einstein and Ben, who were about 20 feet behind.

"You, stay put," Einstein scolded Ben. He ran ahead to catch up.

Carefully, the boys tiptoed toward the clubhouse. As they emerged from the woods, the moonlight outlined their forms.

"I'll start loosening these nails on the roof," Max said. "You guys get ready with the spray paint." Max started ripping out nails.

"That's making too much noise," Einstein cautioned.

Max realized he was right and came around the front to join the others. "Okay, then, let's go in and do our work," he said.

Max lifted the handle to the door and pulled it open. A piece of paper attached to an object hanging from string gently swung at eye level. Ricky flicked his flashlight on and aimed the beam toward it, revealing a small red ball. "Look!" he announced. "It says, *For Max*."

Max reached out for the ball. At the same time, Einstein yelled, "No, Max! Don't touch it!"

It was too late. At the moment Max pulled on the ball, the string triggered a latch that released two plastic buckets, one filled with paint, the other with blueberry jam. The buckets tilted and the boys instantly were splattered from head to toe. "Argh!" they yelled in unison as they turned to run.

Einstein tripped and fell, landing on his backpack that contained a carton of eggs. Ben watched in amazement as his brother frantically tried to wipe egg yolk from his hands. When the boys finally caught up to him, he tried to hide his laughter. They were stained with green paint and dripping with blueberry jam.

17

It had never been easier for Tori to get out of bed on a Sunday morning. She quickly dressed and greeted her father cheerfully at the table. "Hi, Dad, ready for church?"

"Well, sure," Mr. Conroy replied. "Why so excited about church suddenly?"

"Oh, no reason." Tori went about toasting a bagel and pouring juice. Mr. Conroy returned to reading his paper. After breakfast, as they drove to church, Tori was unusually chatty.

Angie and Kelly were waiting at the top of the steps. She bounded up two at a time and they huddled together, chatting in hushed tones. Mr. Conroy greeted the Donovans and Nortons, and the families entered together.

The girls fidgeted in the pew as they got settled. A rash of whispers filled the church, and they noticed people turning their attention toward the entrance doors. Turning around to look, they spied Max and Ricky entering in front of their parents. Their faces were sullen and colored a pale shade of green.

"Look at the boys' faces," Mrs. Donovan whispered. "Are they green? They almost match our dining room walls." The girls tried to suppress giggles. Mr. Donovan suddenly realized the color was an exact match to the dining room paint. He and Mr. Conroy exchanged knowing glances and shook their heads in disbelief.

Let us pray. Church began.

A week passed, and their parents never questioned the girls about what happened. They had been careful to protect the ground around the clubhouse from the paint attack by covering it with plastic so clean-up was quick and simple. Blueberry jam stains still dotted the yard, but the birds and squirrels were making quick work of them.

It was the last Saturday before their ribbon-cutting ceremony and the girls were excited because they finally were ready to paint the inside walls. Almost a week behind on their construction schedule, they were trying hard to make up time. The invitations had been sent out, and Ms. Alvarez had responded that she would be delighted to attend. If they worked hard every day, they could still be ready.

Tori loved painting because she felt like she was creating artwork. Her dad had shown the girls how to use a brush and roller, instructing them to do the ceiling first, followed by the corners, the areas around the trim, and finally the walls. He made a point of reminding them how important it was to clean the brushes each day when they finished. She liked making her mark with the paint, knowing her handiwork would show for years to come. She particularly liked using the roller. The paint seemed to melt onto the wall, leaving a smooth, glistening surface. She thought it was high-tech compared to the regular brushes. She watched the dull drywall transform into the new, clean light green shade, as the steady back-and-forth swish of the roller lulled her into a trance.

"Wow, it's starting to get windy," Angie yelled as she took off after a paper cup that blew over. The other cups toppled, spilling apple juice. One took flight and blew across the field, and Angie chased it down.

Tori snapped out of her daydream. "Boy, it got so windy so quickly. It looks like it's going to rain."

"Darn it, rain will make my hair frizz." Kelly peeked out of the clubhouse to check the clouds.

"Let's put all our equipment away and we can just finish some touch-up paint on the inside," Angie suggested.

The girls cleaned up, worked for about thirty minutes and called it a day.

~ ~ ~

After dinner, Tori was lying with the back of her head on the armrest of her favorite chair with her legs dangling over the other armrest. A pillow propped on her legs served as her desk, supporting a pad of paper. She was working on her speech for the ribbon-cutting ceremony. The TV was on, but she wasn't really watching it. Her father was in the garage, repairing a loose chair leg.

"Let's see...," Tori said out loud, as she considered whom she should thank for helping get their plans off the ground. She jotted names down on her paper.

"This program is being interrupted for an important weather update," an announcer's voice broke into the TV program. A woman wearing a rain slicker appeared on the screen with a satellite map of the eastern United States positioned behind her.

"Dad, come quick!" Tori called. "Something's happening." She walked to the TV, turned up the volume and stood in front of it as he came into the family room, holding the chair leg, and stood by her side.

"This is a severe storm warning for the tri-county region," the reporter said. "Expect wind gusts of up to 80 miles per hour. Flooding may occur in low areas. Stay tuned for updates throughout the evening."

Tori studied the map on the screen. "That's us!" she said as she pulled on her father's shirt sleeve.

"It's okay," Mr. Conroy assured her. "Our house is high enough, it won't get flooded. Let's move any small objects off the porch so the wind doesn't pick them up."

Tori obediently followed her dad to help but remained glum. They got the flashlights out and replaced the batteries in those that needed fresh ones.

"Don't look so worried," Mr. Conroy comforted her. "We're going to be fine. Our house has made it through bigger storms than this one."

Tori suddenly felt selfish. "It's not our house I'm worried about, Dad," she admitted.

"What's the problem, then?"

"It's the clubhouse. What about all our hard work?"

Mr. Conroy realized she had a very real concern. An 80-miles-per-hour wind gust could level the structure in minutes. He gave Tori a hug and told her there was nothing they could do at this point, but wait out the storm and hope for the best.

"Can I call Kelly and Angie?" Tori asked.

"Okay, but if there is any sign of thunder or lightening, hang up, because it won't be safe to be on the phone," he cautioned.

"Okay," she confirmed as she dialed Angie's

number. She needed to hear her friend's voice and wanted to be kept updated on the storm's effect on their clubhouse. She pressed the key for the last number, and the phone began to ring.

After the third ring, she heard Angie answer, "Hello?"

"Angie, it's Tori." She began to feel better, hearing her friend's voice.

The lights flickered, the house became dark, and she heard a soft click as the phone line went dead.

19

Tori could hardly sleep. The wind whipped at the trees, and branches lashed against the side of the house, making strange shadows across the windows. Tired as she was, each thunderclap made her heart pound, keeping her awake. Although she always liked the sound of rain on the roof, this heavy downpour filled her with dread. Somewhere in the wee hours of the morning, she drifted off to sleep.

~ ~ ~

Like the quick flutter of a bird's wings, Tori's eyes opened and closed a few times. The sunlight streaming into her room made it difficult to keep them open. She shaded them with her hand and sat up in bed. Glancing at the clock, which flashed twelve o'clock in steady bursts of neon blue, she remembered the electricity had been out all night.

She went to her jewelry box and fished out her watch. Nine-thirty. She crawled across her bed to look out the window. The world looked like it had been washed clean. The sky was bright blue and the spring grass glistened. But branches and twigs were scattered on the streets and in yards like someone had dropped them from the sky. A sense of urgency filled Tori. The clubhouse!

She ran downstairs to call Angie. No dial tone! Tori raced back up the steps and quickly dressed in blue jeans and a sweatshirt. Without brushing her hair, she put it in a ponytail and called for her father. He was still in bed, exhausted from staying up until the storm blew by. Tori knocked on his door.

"Dad!" No answer.

"Dad!" She knocked harder.

"Hmmm." She heard his half-hearted response.

"Dad, I'm going to Angie's!"

"Uh huh." Silence.

Tori ran down the steps and toward the garage door. After a second thought, she went to the kitchen counter and wrote a quick note:

Dad, went to Angie's. Luv U! T.

20

Tori cut through her neighbors' yards and jogged toward Angie's house, carefully avoiding the twigs and branches that littered the lawns. When she was about halfway there, she saw Angie running toward her.

"Tori!" Angie called out in surprise. "Our phone is out."

"I know, that's why I was coming over. How's the clubhouse?"

Angie stopped when she reached her friend. She let out a big breath. "Not good. About half of the roof came off entirely. It blew about 10 feet and stopped when it hit the trees at the edge of the woods. We're going to have rebuild it."

"I can't believe it."

"We've got a lot of work on our hands."

The girls walked quickly in silence and surveyed the damage. Tori held back her tears. "It's worse than I imagined."

They stared at the damaged structure and decided to meet after church to start repairs.

~ ~ ~

After they had been working for about four hours, Mrs. Donovan came out and suggested they take a break. "Girls, don't overdo it," she said. "Don't you think you've put in enough work for one day?"

"Mom, the ribbon-cutting ceremony is on Saturday," Angie complained. "We won't ever be finished in time."

Mrs. Donovan was about to protest, but she realized her daughter was right. "Okay, one more hour, then call it quits. I'll talk to your dad, and we can try to pitch in to help you this week."

"Thanks, Mom."

Thanks, Mrs. Donovan," Tori and Kelly added.

They finished their work and started to clean up.

What's this? Tori wondered as she found three bent nails in the grass near the corner of the clubhouse. It looked as if the roof nails had been pried from the structure. Very strange.

21

The next day at school, everyone was talking about the storm and comparing stories about what had happened. No one had been hurt, but one girl said her dog's house had blown over. Luckily, the dog was safe inside with the family. Trees had fallen on a student's garage and a teacher's car. The clubhouse roof also was big news.

"Max, did you hear about the girls' clubhouse?" Einstein sat down next to Max and Ricky at the lunch table.

"I heard."

"Well?"

"Well, what?"

"Way to go! It never would have happened if you hadn't pulled those nails out."

"Yeah, thanks," Max replied glumly.

"I thought that was the whole idea," Ricky added, as he pulled a bologna sandwich out of his brown paper bag.

Somehow, every time Max thought about the damage he helped cause, he remembered how he felt the day the boys lost their clubhouse. All their plans and dreams ruined in one pass of the bulldozer.

He shrugged his shoulders. "Sure. Can we change the subject?"

22

The girls couldn't get together until Tuesday to work on the clubhouse. Just four more days until the ribbon-cutting ceremony. They practically ran to Angie's after school, grabbed a snack and got busy trying to repair the roof. Mrs. Donovan joined them, and Mr. Donovan and Mr. Conroy promised to help after work. They listened to their favorite CD and chatted about their plans for Saturday.

Tori noticed that Angie had stopped working and was looking toward the woods. She followed her gaze and spied Max coming toward them. She stopped what she was doing. Kelly continued talking until she realized no one was listening.

Max stopped when he got within a couple yards of the clubhouse. All eyes were on him. He looked at his feet and then toward the girls. "Hi," he said feebly.

"Don't you think you've caused enough trouble?" Angie challenged. "What are you here for?"

"I heard what happened to your clubhouse."

"And now you want to gloat about it?" Tori asked.

"You have every right to be mad at me." Max looked at the ground like he was looking for something he lost. "I thought maybe I could help you out."

The girls looked at Max in stunned silence. "You're kidding, right?" Angie asked.

"No, I'm serious. I know what it feels like to lose a clubhouse, and I think we might have gotten a little out of hand trying to keep you from building yours. I guess that was wrong."

Mrs. Donovan was impressed that Max was brave enough to admit his mistake.

The girls looked at each other to figure out how to react.

"Okay!" Kelly announced. "We need all the help we can get." She went back to hammering and began singing to the music.

Angie and Tori looked at Max, looked at each other again, shrugged their shoulders and together chimed, "Okay."

Tori picked up some nails and handed him a hammer. Pointing to the area where she found the bent nails, she said, "I think you know where these go." Max got to work immediately.

"The nails should be flush with the wood," Tori added. "Just let Angie know when you are done. She's in charge of quality control," she said, winking at her friend.

Angie acknowledged the wink with a knowing smile.

Ben had been hiding in the woods watching the whole episode and couldn't believe his eyes. He ran all the way home and told Einstein, who immediately called Ricky. Both were in shock that their leader had gone over to the enemy's side.

23

Wednesday after school the girls were already at work when Max showed up. Without a word, he picked up a hammer and got busy. The girls were secretly pleased to have Max helping. They were starting to make some real progress.

"Toby!" Angie called out. Her dog was bounding toward the woods. "Toby! Stop! He must be chasing a rabbit." She went running after him.

"Down! Get down!" they heard someone yelling.

"Get your dog off me!" Einstein was pleading as he came running out of the woods with Toby close on his heels.

"Down, Toby," Angie swiftly grabbed the dog's collar to keep him from jumping. "He's just playing, and besides, what are you doing spying on us?"

Ricky came to the side of his friend. "We just wanted to see your silly clubhouse. We heard it was a mess."

"See for yourself," Angie said as she returned

to work.

Einstein's jaw dropped. Ricky looked on with shocked surprise. There was Max helping the girls. And the clubhouse looked great. They didn't know what to say or do. So they just propped themselves against a tree and watched. After about thirty minutes, they stopped work for dinner. Max put his tools away and walked over to join the boys.

"Hi, guys."

"Uh, hi." Einstein replied.

"Fixing the roof," Max said, answering the question he knew was on the boys' minds.

"Right," Einstein said. Ricky just nodded.

The boys headed home together.

~ ~ ~

On Thursday, Max joined the girls once again. Then, to everyone's surprise, Einstein appeared.

"What's up?" Max said.

"Nothin', just thought I'd hang out and watch a little," Einstein answered as he sat down by a tree.

"Why don't you make yourself useful?" Angie suggested and handed him a hammer.

Einstein stood, trying to make up his mind. On one hand, it was against all his instincts to help the girls. But on the other, it seemed like the right thing to do, since he helped cause the damage in the first place. Without saying a word, he walked over to the structure, picked up a handful of nails and pitched in.

About fifteen minutes later, Mr. Ricardo arrived with Ricky, who was carrying a gallon of semi-gloss paint. It was the type of paint the girls needed to finish the trim, but they didn't have enough in their budget to buy it. "Angie, your dad came by the store to buy this for you this afternoon," said Ricky's dad. "I told him it was on me."

"Thanks, Mr. Ricardo!" the girls thanked him enthusiastically.

"And I think my son has something to say to you."

Ricky shuffled his feet and mumbled, "Sorry about the clubhouse."

"And…," Mr. Ricardo coaxed.

"And, I'm here to help."

"Well, jump right in," Tori said.

Ricky started working on painting the trim. Kelly turned up the music. There was an exciting energy in the air. It was contagious as they worked together through the evening, laughing, singing and chatting.

24

"I can't believe it's Friday, our last day to work on the clubhouse," Tori said as she met Angie at the school door.

Kelly came toward them, her backpack hanging over one shoulder. "So, what do you guys want to do this afternoon?"

The girls looked at her in shocked surprise.

"I'm kidding, okay? Just kidding!"

They all laughed and headed to Angie's to get started as soon as possible. Much to their astonishment, Max, Einstein and Ricky were already there, raking the area around the clubhouse. That afternoon, they cleaned the inside, washed the windows and swept the floor. Ricky finished the touch-up painting and Kelly and Einstein planted a few small bushes that Kelly's parents dropped off. Around 6:00, Mrs. Donovan surprised the kids with pizza. Starving, they sat inside the clubhouse on the floor and quickly devoured it.

"I propose a toast," Tori announced. "To the clubhouse!" Everyone raised their soda cans and tapped them together noisily.

"I propose another toast," Max added. "To the girls who built it."

Tori was caught by surprise and grinned. "Here, here!" Angie exclaimed. "To the girls who built it!" Again they tapped the cans together.

Mrs. Donovan came out to remind the kids of the time, and the boys got up to leave.

"Good luck at the ribbon-cutting tomorrow," Max said as he walked toward the door. "See ya on Monday."

"Okay, thanks for helping us out," Angie said. "Bye."

Einstein and Ricky joined their friend and headed for the street.

Kelly and Angie searched Tori's eyes for some guidance.

"Okay," Tori said. She quickly ran out of the clubhouse and called to the boys, "Hey, why don't you guys come tomorrow?"

"Really?" Einstein replied enthusiastically. After a slight pause, he tried to sound less excited. "Well, maybe if we aren't busy."

Max elbowed Einstein in the ribs. "Uh, sure," he said. "We'll be there."

After the boys left, Kelly checked over the list of people who would attend the next day's ceremony, and the girls reviewed everything they would need. Later that night, Tori laid in bed thinking. Her head was swimming with images of the clubhouse, the ruined roof, the boys' clubhouse getting bulldozed, painting the walls, having fun working together, the pizza party. She considered what she would say tomorrow. The thoughts were whirling in her mind. She felt satisfied and tired as she drifted off to sleep.

25

The alarm startled Tori at eight o'clock Saturday morning. She tapped the switch on the clock and laid in bed, wishing for just a few more minutes under the covers. It wasn't often that she got up early on a weekend, but she wanted to make sure she had enough time to practice her speech and prepare for the ceremony. A second alarm chirped from her dresser. *Darn it,* Tori thought. Now she would have to get up to turn that clock off. She crawled to the end of the bed, rolled herself onto the floor and shuffled to the dresser.

"Fine," she scolded the clock as she firmly struck the button to quiet it. "I'm up." She wondered what the day held in store for her. It was pretty outside; that was the first good sign. She dressed in khaki pants, a long-sleeved tee, a vest and hiking boots. After washing her face, Tori rubbed some hair gel in her hands and scrunched her hair to make pretty soft waves that framed her face. She took a last approving look in the mirror. Ready. She went downstairs to join her dad for breakfast.

"Eggs are done!" Mr. Conroy announced. "Are you ready for your big day?"

"As ready as I'll ever be."

"I just want you to know that I'm very proud of you," her dad said as he scooped scrambled eggs onto her plate. "I wasn't sure if you would really do it, but you girls set your mind to building this clubhouse and did a terrific job. I'm particularly proud that, even after you faced several challenges, you just kept at it, and now all your hard work is being rewarded. Congratulations, honey."

"Thanks, Dad. I know I've been spending all my time on that clubhouse, and every so often maybe I overdid it and caused some trouble. It means a lot to me that you are proud of me." She shoveled a huge bite of egg and toast into her mouth and smiled. "I gotta go now." Toast crumbs trickled down her face.

Mr. Conroy laughed, "Now that's my polite little girl. Go ahead, get out of here. I'll see you at eleven."

Tori giggled, wiped her mouth and dashed upstairs to brush her teeth before she ran over to Angie's house.

26

Tori saw Toby sprinting around the backyard at Angie's house. He raced toward her with a welcoming wagging tail.

"Hi, boy!" Tori said as she squatted down next to him and stroked his back. "I think you are as excited as I am."

As she stood up and saw the clubhouse, she smiled with pride. It looked perfect. She waved to Angie, who was putting a tablecloth on a picnic table, then to Kelly, who was reviewing her check sheet.

"Everything looks great," Tori said.

"Thanks, my mom helped me arrange all the paper plates, cups, napkins and drinks," Angie replied.

"Where did the flowers come from?"

"My mom sent them over with me," Kelly smiled. "Aren't they pretty?"

"They're gorgeous!" Tori agreed.

The girls finished arranging the folding chairs and setting the table.

"Someone is here!" Kelly announced.

"Oh my gosh, do you think we're ready?" Tori worried.

"I think we are about to find out," Angie said as she took the plastic wrap off a plate of cookies.

The girls greeted their guests. Kelly checked the names off her list as the others arrived. When everyone was accounted for, she gave Tori and Angie a signal and the three walked to the front of the seating area.

Angie began, "Good morning. Thank you for joining us today to celebrate the completion of our clubhouse."

"We couldn't have done it without the help of our families and support from our friends and neighbors," added Kelly. "Now Tori would like to say a few words, and then we invite you to join us for refreshments and a tour."

Angie and Kelly took a few steps back, leaving Tori in front of the group.

"I wonder if we ever would have taken on this project if we had known how hard it would be to build a clubhouse. I'm glad we did, though, because we learned a lot...but not just how to build it. The first thing we learned about is teamwork.

"Kelly, Angie and I have been friends for years, but we are really different. Angie is very confident and speaks her mind. Kelly is always organizing things and is really into style and fashion. Since I was put in the position of project leader, I began by telling them what to do. I didn't understand why they weren't impressed with how hard I was working at being the leader.

"Finally, I realized that instead of appreciating their differences and discovering their strengths, I was just trying to make them act more like me. Once I understood how important Kelly's organizational skills were and had her take over the scheduling, she was wonderful at keeping us on track. Of course, her fashion sense helped us come up with a very cool interior – even if the walls had to be green. Sorry, Mrs. Donovan, we really do appreciate the paint! And when I actually listened to Angie, I recognized even though she disagreed with me, she was pushing us to get things done the right way, which was not always the easy way. Angie has the confidence to do and say the right thing, not just the popular thing.

"I learned that leading isn't really bossing everyone around. It's discovering what people are good at and helping them do their jobs to the best of their abilities, not just telling them what to do. Thanks to some good advice from my dad, once I started listening more than talking, I became a much better leader. I realized how important our differences are, and how together, we make a terrific team. I heard Ms. Alvarez once say that she worked with a wonderful team, and now I understand what she was talking about. So, I want to thank Kelly and Angie for being special and making this an excellent team."

The guests applauded as Kelly and Angie joined Tori, slipped their arms around each other's waists and smiled at the crowd. A couple cameras flashed, then Tori continued.

"I remember that in my language arts class, 'perseverance' was one of my vocabulary words. It means something like hanging in there when things aren't going so well. I know there's a better definition than that 'cause I remember I got it right on my test." She smiled at her teacher, sitting in the front row, who smiled right back.

"But the point is that Kelly, Angie and I have a whole new understanding of the word. When we started this project, we really didn't know how to build, so this was a huge learning experience. Keeping within our budget seemed impossible, and getting done on time was a miracle. I'm glad we hung in there to get it done. We faced a lot of challenges. Probably the worst was when the storm damaged our roof. It may sound a little funny, but if we didn't have all of those challenges, I don't think we would be as proud today of what we accomplished.

"The third thing we learned about is friendship. The three of us tested our friendship through the long hours we spent together. Sometimes we argued, but we got through just fine. We learned to rely on each other and encourage each other. We learned how to laugh when things got tough, and I think we are better friends than ever before. The big surprise, though, wasn't about our own friendship, it's about the new friends we made." Tori glanced at Max, Einstein and Ricky and caught Max's eye. "Last fall, we had a rivalry with the boys over the old clubhouse that was on the path through the woods."

"Which, by the way, just to make it clear, they didn't win from us, we let them have it," Angie chimed in. The crowd laughed in response, and the boys fidgeted.

"I can't say we've been the best of friends," Tori continued. "I'm not so sure we even thought they were nice. The only time we'd ever been together was when they were throwing blueberries or water balloons at us." Color rose in the boys' faces.

"Well, that's until they faced their own hardship, when their clubhouse was bulldozed to make room for the new neighborhood. I think having gone through something like that made them understand exactly how we felt when the storm damaged our clubhouse. And instead of rubbing it in, they decided to pitch in. Somewhere during the time we worked together, we became friends, and that's a cool surprise. Thanks, guys."

The crowd gave the boys a round of applause.

"So now, we want to thank some very special people."

Kelly stepped forward. "Mom, Dad, thanks for all of your support. Mr. and Mrs. Donovan, we appreciate how you let us hang out at your house all the time, store our equipment and, most importantly, let us build the clubhouse in your field. Mr. Conroy, thanks for pitching in when we needed help and teaching us how to paint. We couldn't have done any of this without you."

Tori continued, "And now we would like to recognize our guest of honor, Ms. Lucinda Alvarez. Would you join us up front, please?" After Ms. Alvarez walked up to stand next to them, Tori told the guests about Ms. Alvarez's interesting background, then continued.

"Everyone needs someone who believes that you can do more than even you thought you could achieve. Ms. Alvarez is that person to us. She never doubted that we could build a clubhouse, even when we doubted ourselves. She took the time to show us what construction is all about. It's not just building a structure, it's about building a part of the community. It could be a research laboratory, an airplane hangar, an office building, or just a simple clubhouse.

"But our clubhouse isn't just a building. It's a place where friends will gather, play games, talk, laugh, sing and plan for the future. She taught us that almost anyone can be successful in construction because there are so many different jobs that are a part of that profession. I don't think any of us even considered construction before this year, and now we can't wait for our next project! Ms. Alvarez, thank you for believing in us, giving us the encouragement to push ourselves a little harder and guiding us along the way. You've become an important part of our lives, and we are dedicating our clubhouse to you." Kelly produced a beautiful bouquet of flowers and handed them to Ms. Alvarez as the guests stood and applauded enthusiastically.

"Now, speaking of our next project," Tori added, "we want to share an idea with you. If three girls, well, that is, three girls with the help of their parents and friends, accomplished building a clubhouse, imagine what we could accomplish with four or five times as many people. Ms. Alvarez told us about an organization called Habitat for Humanity. Through volunteers and donations of money and materials, Habitat constructs or helps fix up houses for low-income families. The new homeowners, called homeowner-partners, help with the work, and the house is sold to the family at an affordable price. The idea is to make it possible for every family to reach its dream of owning a decent home. And I know our families have so many skills to share."

"They make it easy for everyone to participate, no matter how young or old," Angie continued. "Like for kids our age…painting baseboards and doors, or making window boxes."

"Even working on the website, creating newsletters, registering volunteers or making spreadsheets," Kelly added.

"So, along with Ms. Alvarez, we've decided to work with our local Habitat for Humanity affiliate and Youth Chapter this summer and invite you to join us." Tori motioned to a clipboard her friend was holding. "Kelly has a sign-up sheet if you are interested."

There was an awkward silence and Tori didn't know what to do or say next.

Tori's dad raised his hand and said, "You can count me in. Kelly, send that sheet this way, please." Tori smiled and Kelly walked the clipboard over to Mr. Conroy.

Angie's mom spoke up, "After watching you girls this year, I wouldn't miss it."

"And I think I could round up a few supplies,"

Mr. Ricardo joked.

As their guests applauded, the girls announced the end of the program, inviting everyone to tour the clubhouse and have refreshments.

Mrs. B. approached with a beaming smile and a small plant. "You've come such a long way since the day you came home covered in blueberries! Just think how much you accomplished."

"Thanks, Mrs. B. It's been some year, hasn't it?" Tori agreed.

"Your hard work really paid off. Count on some homemade cookies so you can keep a stash in the clubhouse. Now I'm going to take a peek inside."

Tori turned to Ms. Alvarez. "I'm so glad you came!"

"I wouldn't have missed it. I enjoyed your speech. I think you all learned a lot through this experience."

"What do you think of the clubhouse?" Tori asked.

Ms. Alvarez walked around the structure in silence as Tori looked on with a worried expression.

"Quality workmanship, on time and on budget." Ms. Alvarez paused, then smiled at Tori. "I am proud of you. I'd say you have the makings of a successful general contractor."

The two laughed and Tori hugged her. "I can't thank you enough for everything you did for us," she whispered.

Ms. Alvarez handed her a small rectangular package wrapped in white tissue with a gold ribbon. "I have a little something for you three. Why don't you wait to open it later on when you are together?"

Tori took the package, "Thanks, Ms. Alvarez, you didn't have to get us something."

"This has been a wonderful experience for me, too, Tori. It reminds me how fortunate I am to have a job where I look forward to going to work every day."

"Come and get it!" Angie called out from the picnic table where Kelly had just placed a chocolate cake. The two walked over to join the others gathered around the table. Angie handed Tori a slice of cake and she enjoyed a huge forkful.

"Hi." Tori swung around to see Max standing in front of her.

She tried to respond, but instead a burst of cake crumbs fell from her mouth. "Sorry," she mumbled through closed lips.

Max laughed. "That's okay. I just came over to congratulate you and say I'm really sorry about the trouble the guys and I caused. I'm the one who loosened the roof in the first place. That's why it got messed up in the storm."

"I know."

"You knew?"

"Yes, I found the nails you pried out of the roof in the grass the day after the storm."

"We were really dumb."

"Yeah."

"I'm sorry."

"Apology accepted. We appreciated your help."

"You can count on us for that Habitat for Humanity project."

"That's great, Max," Tori smiled. "Why don't you guys come over to the clubhouse next Friday after school and we can start planning."

"Sounds good. I'll ask my folks if I can bring over a pizza or something."

"Cool!"

"Okay, see ya." Max turned to leave.

"Uh, Max," Tori called.

"Yeah?"

"Just don't bring any blueberries, okay?"

"Right."

27

It was one o'clock when the last guest left. The girls' parents were relaxing on the Donovan's porch, having coffee.

"Wow, that was great," Kelly announced.

"Fantastic," Angie confirmed.

"I'm so excited about our summer project," Tori added. "It's wonderful how everyone is supporting it."

She plopped herself on one of the chairs inside the clubhouse and laid her folder on the table. Suddenly, she remembered the package.

"Hey, we have a present from Ms. Alvarez!"

"Why didn't you tell us?" Angie asked excitedly.

"I am telling you. She said to wait until we were all together."

"I love presents," Kelly said with delight.

"Then you can open it," Tori said, handing it to her.

The others watched intently as she carefully unwrapped the package. The tissue protected a shiny brass plate with the inscription:

Built by Girls
Tori Conroy
Angie Donovan
Kelly Norton

Kelly passed it around and they all admired it. "Let's put it up," she suggested.

Angie walked to the corner where their tool box was stashed and took out a ruler, hammer, nail, screwdriver and two screws. They decided to put it directly inside the front door on the wall. Kelly made a quick measurement and two pencil marks where the screws would go. Angie tapped the nail lightly with the hammer to get the holes started for the screws. Kelly positioned the plate, and Tori placed the screws in the holes, then tightened them. The plate was in place in minutes.

"Perfect," Angie announced.

"Awesome," Kelly agreed.

Tori put down her tools. "We make a great team, don't we?"

"I wonder what kind of project we will put our names on next?" Kelly said.

They considered the question as they admired their handiwork.

Tori smiled and thought to herself, *the sky's the limit!*

THE END

MEET LINDA ALVARADO
- the inspiration for the character
"Lucinda Catalina Alvarez"

I use my full name, not just my initials, on the plaques that are placed on the buildings I construct, because I want people to know it was a woman who built them.

When Linda Alvarado was a little girl, she dreamed of building high-rises. Today, as President and CEO of Alvarado Construction, Inc., Linda lives her dream.

Her company is a Construction Management, Commercial General Contractor, Development and Design/Build firm based in Denver, Colorado, with offices in Arizona, New Mexico, California and several other states. The company specializes in commercial, retail, industrial, government, environmental and transportation contracts and has successfully constructed multi-million dollar projects throughout the United States and Latin America including high-rise office buildings, convention centers, aquariums, airports, schools, healthcare facilities, stadiums, prisons, restaurants and technology centers.

Born in Albuquerque, New Mexico, Linda grew up with five brothers. As the second youngest, she says,

"It was a lot of fun and very competitive. Athletics were important, and we played many different sports. When there are six kids in a family, you have a team! Playing sports with my brothers enabled me as a young girl to feel comfortable in non-traditional environments. I learned to not immediately give up when I struck out, knowing that I would get another turn at bat. I was able to develop a level of comfort to take some risks and began to try new things that girls had not done before. My parents always encouraged me to pursue my goals and dreams. I am grateful that their expectations for me were the same as for my brothers."

Linda's mother, Lily Sandoval Martinez, is a Hispanic woman born in New Mexico. When Linda was born, she managed the household without having running water, took in ironing to earn money, and hauled water from the drainage ditch to wash the family's clothes. She had a very positive attitude and wanted to make sure that her daughter was not discouraged from accomplishing things simply because she was female.

Luther Martinez, Linda's father, was born in California. He hauled firewood to sell, worked as a delivery driver for a music company, and later was an equipment inspector for the Department of Energy. Both of Linda's parents grew up speaking Spanish. They believed that a strong focus on educational achievement and learning English were important to the success of their children.

In the early 1960's, when she was in fifth grade, her school had a Sports Day competition, and Linda wanted to participate in the high jump. She had been high jumping for a long time in her backyard, and her older brothers had all competed, but the school would not allow a girl to compete.

Her mother took Linda to visit the principal and find out why they would not allow her to participate. The principal explained that it would be inappropriate for a girl to compete because "girls wore dresses and the rules said, 'no girls.'"

"I was proud my mother and father showed me that it was okay to challenge rules in a respectful way, and to believe that even though a rule or tradition exists today, it doesn't have to be that way forever," says Linda.

Linda did get to compete in the high jump that year. A thin little girl, she was the shortest in the field of 30 boys. Much to the surprise of everyone, she won the event! To her it was wonderful. Others reacted with mixed attitudes. Some were very excited. Others thought a girl shouldn't be doing that and were shocked. But it enabled Linda to be more competitive in athletics and eventually better in business. "From participating in sports, I learned about developing winning strategies, focusing on acquiring new skills, team-building and risk-taking – all of which are important in managing a business." She still has the ribbon from the high jump competition.

Through Linda's perseverance and her parents' encouragement, girls divisions in high jumping and hurdles were opened at her school, and soon after, in many schools.

In keeping with breaking non-traditional roles, Linda also made history as the first Hispanic owner (male or female) of a major league baseball franchise. As a partner of the Colorado Rockies Baseball Club, her role is also significant as it marked the first time that any woman entrepreneur was involved in a bid for ownership of a major league team.

Linda has been the focus of many articles in the media, books, business publications and educational texts, and has been featured on the cover of several national magazines. She has set high standards as a business owner, and her accomplishments have opened doors for others to pursue new career possibilities.

In addition to managing her business, she is a leader in civic and business organizations and is the recipient of numerous awards. She is a corporate director of 3M, QWEST Communications, Lennox International, Pepsi Bottling Group and Pitney Bowes. She was a founding member and the first woman elected as Chairman of the Board of the Denver Hispanic Chamber of Commerce and served as Commissioner of the White House Initiative for

Hispanic Excellence in Education.

A recipient of the Horatio Alger Award in 2001, Linda also was named one of the "100 Most Influential Hispanics in America" by *Hispanic Business Magazine* in 1998. She was honored in New York, along with U.S. Attorney General Janet Reno and poet laureate Maya Angelou, as a recipient of the prestigious Sara Lee Corporation Frontrunner Award for exemplary achievement and leadership. Her success in business and active community involvement have led to her recognition as a trailblazer in her field.

In 2003, Linda was inducted into the National Women's Hall of Fame in Seneca Falls, New York. She was twice selected as the United States Hispanic Chambers of Commerce Business Woman of the Year and was named the SIFE Revlon Business Woman of the Year. In addition, she has received the Martin Luther King Social Responsibility Award, and the National Association of Construction Enterprise Hardhat Award for Outstanding Woman in Construction.

A nationally recognized speaker, she has given keynote presentations for corporations, institutions of higher education, national conferences, and in public schools, motivating young people to excel and achieve their dreams.

ASKED MS. ALVARADO:

WHAT IS A GENERAL CONTRACTOR?

A General Contractor is a problem-solver, someone who knows how to represent the interests of the owner and the project subcontractors and suppliers. A general contractor must have the ability to develop positive solutions to resolve design and construction issues between architects, owners and local building departments. She or he is responsible for the overall management of the project from start to completion and coordinates all the building trades to assure the structure is built according to the architectural blueprints and project specifications, and in compliance with building codes.

The general contractor manages the master schedule, workforce activities, subcontractors, quality control inspection and safety programs. Specific elements of the work include survey, installation of foundations and concrete, erection of the structural framing, as well as specialty work such as fire protection and security. The general contractor also hires all subcontractors including electrical, mechanical, excavation, landscaping firms and others

116

to perform interior finish work including wood trim, flooring, paint and signage.

WHAT IS THE MOST FASCINATING JOB YOU HAVE ACCOMPLISHED?

It is hard to pick just one. Invesco Field (The Denver Broncos Stadium), Colorado's Ocean Journey Aquarium, and the Phoenix Convention Center have all been large and challenging projects.

Recently I undertook the restoration of a historic landmark constructed in 1921. It was the original courthouse in Denver, a beautiful 3-story brick structure that had been abandoned for more than thirty years. Alvarado Construction redeveloped and renovated the building, designing and reconstructing it to provide office and meeting space for eleven community non-profit organizations.

The building was rededicated as the Bernard Valdez Hispanic Heritage Center. Alvarado Construction considers this project to be a "labor of love." It is important that our firm is involved in projects like this that assist others in the community to also have an opportunity to succeed.

WHAT KINDS OF JOBS ARE AVAILABLE IN CONSTRUCTION?

The design and construction of a project takes a team of people with different expertise. There are many jobs available, such as architects, engineers, interior designers, project managers, carpenters, cement masons, surveyors, excavators, superintendents, electricians, plumbers, drywall installers, office

117

engineers, scheduling engineers, safety officers and quality control managers, just to name a few.

ARE THE ROLES FOR WOMEN IN CONSTRUCTION GROWING?

There were no female role models in this industry when I started. If women were on construction sites at all, they were secretaries. Today, I have several women engineers and project managers working for me. I get great satisfaction from this, not just personally, but in the fact that women are now beginning to be involved in designing and constructing everything from landscaping to skyscrapers, hospitals, homes and manufacturing facilities. Knowing that women can succeed in this industry is an important step forward in providing more career choices to young girls.

WHAT KIND OF EXPERIENCE IS VALUABLE IN THE CONSRUCTION FIELD AND OWNING A COMPANY?

Both formal education and actual experience on a construction site are very important in the construction industry. It is not just knowing the basics about building a structure; you must have specific knowledge of construction requirements. Math skills are critical, as are close attention to details and a focus on producing the highest quality work delivered on-time and in-budget. Operating a successful business requires an understanding of finance and control of cash flow, hiring, training, motivating, and supervising people, business development, risk management, marketing, insurance, community relations and many other aspects. Important work experience is also gained on the jobsite learning the day-to-day process, coordination and communication. There may be opportunities to work during college through internships with design or construction firms. You can also enroll in educational programs conducted by the building trades associations. Useful degrees include Construction Management, Engineering and Business.

WHAT ADVICE DO YOU HAVE FOR GIRLS?

Even when you experience setbacks, you cannot let other people discourage you from focusing on achieving your hopes and dreams. Get the necessary formal education. Learn the basic skill sets in your particular field that are necessary to succeed. Take some risks, but also have some fun. You can achieve your dreams!

As a little girl, I dreamed of building high-rises, and today, I do.

GIRLS KNOW HOW® thanks Ms. Alvarado for telling us about her experience in commercial general contracting. Remember, these ideas are just to get you thinking about opportunities, and are based on one successful woman's experience. So, if you would like to learn more, do some research in the library, search websites, talk it over with your parents, or ask a teacher or guidance counselor at school.

 AND

Vist www.girlsknowhow.com
email books@nousoma.com or
call 610.458.1580 for more information

EXPLORING CAREERS

When I grow up, I would like to be a:

1._____

2._____

3._____

If I could have any job, I would be a _____

Describe why you would like this job (For instance: I like to
be active, I'm good at math or science, I like to read or write.
I like adventure, travel, helping people, it pays a lot.)

1._____

2._____

3._____

Whom do I know personally that has a job in this field?

_____

Is there anyone famous who has this type of job?

_____

What will I need to do this job well? (check all that apply)

_____ Good grades

_____ High school education

_____ Some college or more school after high school

_____ A special skill (what is it?)_____

_____ Special training (what kind?)_____

_____ Other_____

How can I learn more about this job?

____ Get a book from the library

____ Interview someone who has this job

____ Research this profession on the Internet
       (with parents' permission)

____ Spend a day at work with someone who has this job

____ Look for what kind of jobs in this field are listed in the
       newspaper employment section

I PLEDGE TO LEARN MORE ABOUT
CAREER OPPORTUNITIES

List what you will do to learn more about this job:

1. This week, I will_____

2. This month, I will_____

3. Next month, I will_____

Signed_____ Date_____

Design the Clubhouse of Your Dreams!

Sketch the outside or interior plan of your own special hideout or gathering place.